San Luis

San Luis

Justin Lowe

PUNCHER & WATTMANN

© Justin Lowe 2024

This book is copyright. Apart from any fair dealing for the purposes of study and research, criticism, review or as otherwise permitted under the Copyright Act, no part may be reproduced by any process without written permission. Inquiries should be made to the publisher.

First published in 2024
Published by Puncher & Wattmann
PO Box 279
Waratah NSW 2298

info@puncherandwattmann.com

A catologue record for this book is available from The National Library of Australia.

ISBN   9781923099371

Cover image by Judy Lowe
Cover design by David Musgrave

Printed by Lightning Source International

To my brother-in-law, Graeme, my dear friend these many years who, for reasons known only to himself, chose to marry into the adventure.

Contents

9	Evening with my Father
11	Life Suite
11	1) The Guinea Pigs
16	2) Bomb Threats
18	3) Looking Up
20	Binisafua
21	The Transition
22	The Lake
23	Iron Lady
24	Wuthering Heights
25	The Anchor
26	Whale Song
27	Francis Fukayama
28	Visions of a Strawman
29	Dr. Chekhov
31	The Prospector
32	Dirty Poker
34	Moree
36	Wilcannia
37	Hestia
38	Charles Simic
40	The Publican
41	Ruth
42	The Quiet Corner
43	The Runner
44	Clytemnestra
46	Ladders
47	Palazzo Ducale, 1349
48	Lake Tiberius
50	Lost Dog in the Brownstones
51	Leatherjacket
52	The Poet Imbibes
53	Suburbia

54 Fire Stairs
56 On the Frontier
58 From the Wilderness
59 Fitzgerald
60 1920
61 Madame Curie
63 Aides-de-Camp
64 Newsreel Ken
66 Palimpsest
68 Still
69 Mount Lofty
70 The Seamstress
71 The Governess
73 St. Kitts
74 An Open Book
76 The River Man
86 The Lost Parable

87 Acknowledgements

Evening with my Father

come dusk
life would spill over the edges
and his voice would go low,
guttural,
like the wind in a cornfield

he'd just
purse his lips a little
murmur "Adeline, oh, Adeline"
let his eyes go glassy
as he sipped his wine

and watch the cockatoos
screech and careen
on the wires
plumed acrobats drunk
on the possibilities

he would watch them
and pat me
softly on the knee
and laugh
that little inner laugh of his

not a chuckle,
that poor cousin of derision,
but like the light had ticklish fingers,
and the neighbours would wave
through their pearly gate smiles

and my little dog
would growl
the way he would
at hawkers
of all things ghostly and corporeal

and lick my father's hand
as though
reminding him
that all that mattered
was right here

and then the clouds
would blush like china dolls
and a slow hush
would descend
on the gully

and the children
playing in the park
would lift like the breeze
and each object
suddenly radiant

in that teeming hour
when the lorikeets
pip
death will come
between the wires

and the kookaburras
laugh
at the dying of the light

Life Suite

1. The Guinea Pigs

I.

I was adopted
by two loving but impulsive people

my younger sister
was likewise adopted into a kind of summer storm

in that era
a single woman lost all rights to her child

unless that woman possessed
unearthly powers of persuasion

we were both strangely blessed
by a cold reckoning.

II.

on that drive home the first day
my mother fretted about the sun on my face

pleaded with my father
to go home a different way

he just remembered me sleeping:
it was the beginning

of my long love affair with the sun
and with a laugh my father directed only at my mother.

III.

two years later my sister arrived.
she cried so much

I pleaded with my parents
to take her back. a familiar trope.

but pretty soon
I was in love with her too

she followed me everywhere
a little toothless dumpling with toilet brush hair.

IV.

when my sister had just started to speak
my mother whisked us off to Spain

to Franco's Spain
to the island that held out longest for the Republic

garrisoned by pimply conscripts
and punished through neglect

we had our water delivered by mule
there was a spring down the road

where I collected bottled water
still bear the scar from running on the cobbles

my mother painted vast oils
always of streets

narrow streets
leading to a vanishing point

almost as though
she could already see to the end of her short life

my sister and I
learnt to read and write in Spanish

we were as fluent as children can be
who fear the nuns' petty cruelties

they loathed our mother
and all she stood for

the same arid worldview
that wrenched us from our birth mothers' arms

my father brought gifts and news of home
left sobbing like the wind in the well.

V.

in the nearest town, San Luis,
it seemed every woman over thirty

wore nothing but black, silently
genuflecting at the crossroads

war was everywhere
the scars and void of war

you could see the fresh plaster
covering over the bullet holes

the black-clad women, heads down
waiting for the conscripts to leave the butcher's the baker's

VI.

on the far side of town
on the sleek army road to Mahon

there was a clinic
run by an English doctor

an expert in facial reconstruction
a plastic surgeon

his patients were mostly victims
of that vast tragedy

for which the Spanish
was merely a rehearsal

men by now in their 40's and 50's
with featureless faces and pits for eyes.

VII.

the Hawker Hurricane
had an unfortunate propensity to catch fire

and for its cabin latch
to seize up at certain altitudes

I will spare you the details
other than to say

each new war
finds new ways to be cruel

to my eternal shame and regret
I used to stare at those kind gentle men

as they sunned themselves
outside the baker's in San Luis

benga benga!
my mother would scold me

as though trying to herd me away
from the mad dog the midday sun

2. Bomb Threats

I.

after Spain
I attended an all boy's school in Sydney
from age 10 to 18

perched high on a hill
like some grim Norman watchtower
the long shadows that seeped into your bones

fingers of mist on the winter playing fields
Wilfred Owen, boiled cabbage
and matron's antiseptic all conflated

to instil in a ten year old boy
a crippling and indelible
propensity for nostalgia

II.

in the 1970's
the Brezhnev years had spread
their grey tentacles all the way to us

everything seemed broken under leaden skies
run down rusted vandalised
it was as though

with the looming spectre of The Bomb
no-one could see the point
of fixing anything

people smoked as though lined up against a wall

the teachers smoked the boys smoked
my mother my father my sister smoked
even the school chaplain after morning prayers

there was
this permanent oil slick on the harbour
the sun painted tiny rainbows on each morning

we wore suits and ties and straw hats
like little cupie dolls of power
we wondered where the world was we would inherit

III.

if the sirens sounded
we were told
we had three minutes to find shelter

our desk as good a place as any

there to await the blinding flash
the searing heat that would
somehow miraculously save us from ourselves

and if the school bell rang mid-period
as it seemed to do quite often in the 1970's
we were told to leave our things

assemble calmly
across the street from the placard-wavers
the gauntlet we had to run each morning

bide our time before the all-clear
trying to guess
which kerb-side Cassandra rang it through

3. Looking Up — for Robert Adamson

perhaps
the most surprising thing
about this job
      is the birds

no two days the same
all the ills of the world
a puzzle always in need of solving
      but I can always count on the birds

you think
I'm talking about poetry
don't you:
      I'm talking about the birds

in a car park at Narellan
a stand of river gums
lining the Georges catchment
      galahs shriek their joy to be birds

eolophus roseicapilla;
while I pack the COVID bags
separate the serums from the swabs
      I smile at the gum nut rain of the birds

all the ugly noise drowned out
by joy
at the tiers of changing light
       I bin my gloves and laugh with the birds

in Bankstown
when the days grow longer
under the wheeling clouds of starlings
       the doctors ask have I seen the birds

the Cockatoo mobs
over the Ingleburn estates
treading rusty roofs with an air of ancient cunning
       shrug, look at him off smiling at the birds

I do my job
amongst the poor
the sick and the frail
       and amongst the birds

under the eagle's shadow
on the M5 heading north
maybe the loudest bird of them all
       a kind of silent hammer blow

Binisafua

on just such an occasion as this
the boy spies his face in a rock pool

the wind makes it dance
and his laughter lifts a curtain of gulls

meanwhile a ship weighs anchor in the narrow cove
disgorges its grim cargo from Alicante

red lobsters snapping at each other
in the simmering pot of their affluence

shipping tycoons and war-profiteers
returned to the scene of their first triumph

the cliffs behind are a wedding cake pumice
up which they climb along a narrow path

trailed by a fat Eurydice
bone-white under a jet-black parasol

the boy chews the end of his snorkel
and watches them climb

to where his mother waves her slender arms
like the windmills on the flat road to San Luis

and the wind whistling in the cypress pines
and the windmill groan of those fat Germans climbing

becomes one of his most cherished most desolate sounds

The Transition

up there
the dirge has already begun.

all day
I have been listening to the sound.

I am all ears
and a coat billowing like a rumour.

they are banging ladles
against pots.

both articles sit awkwardly
in their lily-white hands,

like babies holding a gun.

I am listening to the soft autumn rain
and the sound of I know not what.

a carp breaks the water
but that isn't it.

they are perched on the rise,
jutting their glass jaws at the echo of their own displeasure.

they bang pewter against tin
and wonder who will calm the dogs

now the servants have all vanished with the silver.

The Lake

the sigh of an empty playground
too near the moon
and the owl's limpid eye
watching them pass round the bottle
cup the autumn mist in their cobweb fingers

this is how bad marriages begin
unhappy children breed unhappy children
this is the seat of power, right here
like the obverse of an ancient coin
Minerva and her owl's eyes
looking down from the smart houses on the rise

while the shallow laughter of the lost
dances fleet foot across the water

Iron Lady

the regime proved predictably short-lived
a night maybe two and then the familiar pop of a cork
all the neighbourhood dogs mistook for a gun shot
this was in the days before the moral compass got nationalised
before the wallpaper started peeling in austerity's rising damp
and all the ancient cracks reappeared
so much had happened so much dust still hung in the air
it was a simple matter to blame your clouded judgement on events
claim as little victories what were in fact a series of slow capitulations
thus one seemingly innocuous nightcap became a week-long bender
and the landlady was far too old to be anything but kind
and anyway she had seen it all, or so she said
and so was all too easily distracted by some ingenuous question
such as the one about gaslit streets and a proliferation of cutthroats

but perhaps the cruellest trick of all was the one played by the light
when during that last great "pea-souper" you glimpsed
in an all too brief moment of clarity your face reflected
in a tea room window so caked with grime and nicotine
that you looked like the marble bust of an emperor
gazing gimlet-eyed at a world it no longer recognised
that seethed around you blindly as around some point
forever frozen in time and space

Wuthering Heights

when the chapters of your life no longer morph
one into the other, but
stand like plinths in some misty field
listing the names of battles won and lost

in different wars in different countries for disparate causes,

when the drums roll with the mist
over the tactless moorlands of some oblique regret
to some frozen lake where sound carries clear, far too clear,

and the metaphor tires of you now,
leaves you to your evasions,
to the dog-eared version of your life already a thrift store yellow,

journeyman.

The Anchor

fear is the simplest, the most cost-effective,
the black gold of our craft.

anger takes some effort
a little less than sadness, a lot less than jealousy

but an effort all the same,
with mixed rewards.

none are quite as elaborate
as the mousetrap of nostalgia

best set and forgotten in some dark corner of a room
the haunted forest of sepia on the mantle.

no, friend, fear is a much quicker sell.

all it takes to send fear rippling
is to stand facing the wrong way in a crowded elevator,

whistle "Waltzing Matilda" on a peak hour bus
(fear is everywhere on the morning commute)

or better still, simply
stand and point at an empty corner of the sky:

you can stop whole cities this way

Whale Song

last night I joined a gang.
a group of hooded spectres said:
"grandpa, would you like to join us?"
and so I did. there was a ruffling of feathers as we shook.

they mulled verbs like half-cooked dough
in the pale fire of their insouciance.
they flicked their hands at nouns
I had lived in all my days.

they asked: "grandpa, when did wars begin?"
they asked: "grandpa, why did you chew up the world?"

they circled the fire with their hooded heads bowed
as though traversing a narrow ledge.

I wanted to apologise but I could not.
the dream sewed my mouth shut.
I hummed like a moth in the pale light of their questions.

for the old to apologise to the young
requires an act of Parliament, a Papal Bull.
thus I deflected like the old do with their soft skin.

like when the first whale decided
that the sea was a far safer option
and so returned to where their songs carried farthest.

Francis Fukuyama

there was a short interlude
then night again
and oblations
and candles lit at makeshift altars

and an orchestra tuned its strings
for some dissonant elegy
while the dancers limbered up for Britney
and teenagers pouted into their father's silverware
while their Nokias pinged in the dinner time shoe box

there was a short interlude from
when a flock of geese could trigger a war
and the threat of violence was so vast
it was almost metaphysical

to when I still don't know what happens next

Visions of a Strawman

and the mass ranging from apprehension to terror
as always: only heightened by some others
crossing in serried ranks an invisible border

cautious of the strange fauna, the night sounds
wasting precious ammunition on the glint
of moonlight in a farmer's grotto

and the cities emptied of the leaders and the leaderless
the myopic of heart and soul run to the hills
that echo with their wasted buckshot

and the names slowly crossed off a list
these others brought with them
a long list of those who spoke up

who dared to mark this day red letter
and were neither flattering or blithe in their appraisal
and now shown a pen and paper and asked to sign

and those who signed shot anyway
alongside those whose principles
rendered them briefly illiterate

and all of them erased
their names their words their deeds
no heroes no martyrs no graves to garland

just the blank of a bully's face
as his blows hit home:
kookaburras laughing at the ships unloading

Dr Chekhov

it was a condition
little understood at the time.

a stigma surrounded it,
for nature abhors a vacuum

and back then
stigmas were easily procured.

the symptoms varied,
often depending on the mood of the observer.

papers had been written
but were yet to be peer-reviewed

for it was only manifest in the provinces
and no-one would venture far from the capital.

in its most severe cases
the patient was reported to lose all hope,

reduced to single syllables like a newborn,
their eyes turned the startled blue of a newborn,

the shallow breath of the hopeless.

in milder cases
patients would confuse the ceiling with the floor

east with west
day with night, etc
they would become agitated
at the sound of laughter the twitter of birds

and if not tied down
they would prowl the night like foxes.

the only deaths from this affliction
came by accident, mostly falls in the night

the deep pits dug by fellow-sufferers
who discovered life has a strong hold

and though the coroner was kept very busy
the records remain sketchy

and we rely now on eyewitness accounts
mostly from relatives

who authorities suspect
may have been prone to embellishment

with one eye on compensation.

The Prospector

when the axe in your hand
stops feeling heavy
you should probably lay it down gently

when her laughter rasps
like the key that fits
a little too easily

go stare
at your pale face
in the river

when the time devoted
and the glitter in your pan
become your only talking point

walk away walk away, go back to the city friend

when courage and faith
become synonymous
sniff the wind for fire or the damp armpits of the orator

look for sharks on the dawn tide
like you look for mice in the threshing
calmly and deliberately with no blackness in your soul

Dirty Poker

though
I had heard the belch
of his rusty sidearm cranking
I mistook it for cattle
lost in the bracken
sick on clover

and though
that rank odour of damp muslin
I should have recognised
from all those nights
holed up together
in that alpine shack

watching
the other man's thoughts
dance like semaphore
in the half-light
of the ever-dying
fire

I did not
and I did not
heed
the absence of birds
the dusk clotting
in that great wounded sky

with no mopoke
to mourn it
I did not
though
I spied some
cold ash on the lip

of our
first fruitless dig
and something
living in there
that let out a sudden shriek
like metal striking quartz

a sound
that dashed all plans
of waiting out the night there
nestled
with my sleeping hope
and so

we circled round and round
in a world leeched of sound
feeling out the absence of each other
with our noses and our ears
like blind dogs circling the yard
on a length of rotten old rope

they had both chewed through long ago

Moree

I worry about my nephew.
I worry about a lot of things
but now and then I worry about my nephew.

he is a man of twenty-nine
who long ago had my measure,
so he's fine.

but all the same I worry.

when I heard about Moree I worried.
some job on a cotton farm
on the treeless expanse among the sickly rivers.

I stood at my window for a long time
looking west, as it happens
due west where the day dies.

it is, after all, what the anxious do,
like all the well-meaning and ineffectual of this world,
we stare at glass

our breath clutching like a fist.

I know my nephew loves me
and that he has my measure
but he hides the best of himself from me

he hides his fears and worries from me
which is where all his courage lies
and so I can't quite get a fix and I worry.

I try to picture Moree:
the taut sky
the vast plains and silted rivers

the cotton
that sucks it all dry
like a vast white sponge

and then I worry again:
that he won't take his warfarin
that the heat will pound on his heart until it breaks

I wanted to write a poem today about nature
because it is to nature we turn when we worry
but all I could see was a vast emptiness

and so

Wilcannia

a woman stands by a river.
she stands as though perplexed by it
by the very fact of it

not how to ford it or how fast
it is flowing or why or whether
the river is rising or falling

she stands there straight-backed
rubbing her chin as though wondering
whether the river could bear the weight of her

the way it carries her reflection
and that of the swans lighting on it
bearing night under his left wing her right

the woman stands there just long enough now
to cause this poem concern
she stands there so long gazing

at her stark reflection
in the inexorable flow of dark waters
that this poem feels a sense of urgency rising in it:

that there is more to the world
than this mild conceit
the poem is unaware

Hestia

I leave at first light
and return to a mausoleum.

I bring some figment of the world back with me
like the bared teeth of that trash bin puppy.

as I shake off the scuttlebutt
a plate shifts on the drying rack

a floorboard creaks as though
something had run off ahead of me

looking in every room of my house
dimpling the sofa that only the sun sat on briefly,

deciding whether or not it will stay.

Charles Simic — for Kristen "Krip" Cherry *

I.

Dear Charles. Thank you for the games of chess:
I still owe you one ivory tiger.

Thank you for pulling me from that dark pond:
insomniacs seem to make reluctant heroes.

You pulled me out and whispered something in my ear
a little canticle of nonsense, or maybe Serbian;

I am not very good with languages,
or epistles, it would seem.

II.

You often whisper when I am a little lost, Mr Simic,
like a well-oiled door opening onto a warm room

where there is bread baking in an oven
and a girl with heavy breasts kneads dough,

and your old pal Ristovic raises a glass
and watches the girl while a T-train rattles past the window.

III.

You have seen me through some good times and some bad, Charles,
but mostly bad because that's when we call on our muses,

the dripping tap days in a room full of echoes,
fevered while the cold gnaws at you like a monstrous rat.

IV.

But there have been the plush days too,
the warm bread smell of her as I stirred the covers

and the light breaking through
where her face melted onto the pillow

as I read you to her
and as she lay on her side

a single tear rolled down, a morning tear,
like the last star falling.

V.

Thank you, Mr Simic, for reminding me of her
who no longer lives and breathes like your poems,

and of the trees so still they seem afraid of themselves
and of the Spirit that is nowhere and everywhere.

* This poem borrows lines from "Romantic Landscape" by Charles Simic (from "A Wedding in Hell")

The Publican

my friend looks tired
I mean really tired
I have never seen him drag his feet like this

when I say he's my friend
he's really the man who pours my wine
but he's also a friend

wine does strange things to people
he and I, for instance,
should never have been friends

but now I worry about him:
his face is all puffed up
like one big tear

sometimes I see my face
refracted in my glass
and I look old, so old, older than First Principles

much older than the glass, or the wine
but no older than my friend
the publican

who could have been my son in another life

we live too much
of this world within us
I sigh, and he nods

it is summer
so he opens his doors to the world
he may be the bravest man I know

Ruth

I was bled according to custom.
it rained unseasonably when I bled,
not before or after, just during.
so each morning and night
the old women would run their calloused hands
through my hair, feeling for the tell-tale bumps.

when I opened the gate
the cows would come to me
as they would come to anyone
in the dry season
their shanks all bloody from the jackals.

but this, too, was taken as a sign.
when the swallows nested in the thatch
as they did each summer,
this was taken as a sign.
when the cock crowed at the butter moon

when the river bed spelt out
certain letters in the baked mud
an acrostic of curses
because my skull was too tiny for horns
when we butchered our enemies

and they butchered us in turn
when the orphans
were ferried away by white angels
and returned many years later
straight-backed with a cruel pride

all this was taken as a sign,
something cruel and deliberate running through my veins.

The Quiet Corner

the garish shrine I understand.
or, at least, it does not unsettle me.

with the plastic Dinesh or a fat Siddharta blinking
like stars through the Bodhi tree,

or Mary mother of God
slow-clapping the flaws of the world.

the candy-cane incense
catches me mid-step every time,

but it does not worry me
as much as the staring stone-cold effigy,

dark eyes fixed on me as I explain
to some deaf old dear why I am here

for her little blue cap of gore and effluvia
without the good grace to even take off my shoes

waving my lanyard like rosary.

and though I nod to the quiet corner
it is less out of deference than fear,

for I have seen what mischief
the little gods make

The Runner

and so he performs his oblations
at the dry stream
slings his mother's goatskin gourd
and the birds chase him

their beaks snapping at his ears
their wings snapping like sardonic applause.

he runs as though hunted
deliberate and steady as thunder
running up into the hills
where the birds form a parliament

in the high branches
of cypress pine and boxwood
the wind whistling up there
carrying the sad news from the beacons

to which he runs without thinking
like a moth blind as light
like some hunted thing
like those birds chasing tomorrow's carrion

Clytemnestra

those
gleaming vessels
of fate

the well-lived
the sanctified

bestowed
the luxury
of a death off-stage

a servant's scream
from the wings

those parvenus
who don't
carry wallets

fall
like leaves
from a tree

autumn
ruffles their hair
with a sigh

a sigh
passed like champagne
on the waiter's tray

while light
tinkles everywhere
in the tiny bubbles so busy dying

in the candles
snuffed out later
by invisible hands

Ladders

I had feathers this morning
they scratched like the sheets
of a slow-emptying bed
until they shed
with the mist and the claxton
of the bower bird

and the pith of the day
was whetstone
that housed a shriek
and it tripped Sisyphus on his way
to some easy money

and I was
ten rungs up a ladder
when my feathers peeled away
and Sisyphus nodded as he passed
blind to my distress
whistling the kind of tune you know
will prick the ear of a God or two

Palazzo Ducale, 1349

that people would rather die
than risk a trip to the hospital

risk their names being entered
in the great ledger there

where the soldiers
who still march through their dreams

could easily find them
and that their names are entered anyway

afterwards

all this probably confirms the decision
of the Council of Ten whose ledger it is

to offer them refuge
from whatever footfalls in the night

still haunt them
that they would rather die

than risk that trip
deaf to the irony

pounding on the Four Doors

Lake Tiberius

Menelaus, my friend,
you could not have written
at a worse time.

if I seem ungrateful
it is because last night's frost
like the breath of Eurydice,

has cracked
a whole day's work
fresh from the kiln

(shelved
as you know
on our old day beds, friend)

your mother's urn among them,
all garbage now
for the gods to rummage through.

but that,
my dear Menelaus,
is not even the worst of it,

for the boy
who tended the fire,
believing it was somehow his fault,

has fled into the night -
last seen running for the hills
draped in meagre cotton from my mother's loom

(fit
for a firewatcher
but not for the hills)

and the jackals
are no longer afraid
of our dogs

Lost Dog in the Brownstones — for all the victims of COVID-19

once upon a time
there was a grey dog
with one brown eye one blue
like something trapped between earth and sky

he had everything to live for
this grey dog with his elemental eyes
answered to no-one, told everyone their business
knew the streets far better than the streets deserved

he ate six seven maybe eight good meals a day
slept in the nooks with the truth tellers, finders of lost pennies
stood Sphinx-like while the drunk banker
wept for a good half-hour into his grey mane

and then the soft spring coughed
and the pavements shivered
and each slow line of hearses
purred like black kittens in the rain

Leatherjacket — for Robert

they come to me
like a lender of last resort.

at the four stations of life
they come knocking,

looking for words to salve
or light the glooming,

like light's jumbled mores off the mulloway shoals
where the flood waters bruise the bay,

they come looking for words
that they mumble every day,

just not in the right order.

so who, then, finds the words
at the poet's passing?

The poet imbibes

something happened a long way from here
and long long ago

no witnesses
the echo died out in the void

some owl hooted some pale stars blinked
there was a muffled sound that quickly soughed into the earth

it had to happen:
nothing would be the same if it hadn't

don't look at me like that

these words may never have found each other
space and time might have even drifted apart

what do you know anyway?

the two need an event
like a fraught couple needs a child

something happened, is all I'm saying
some tree fell in the dark forest

and no-one heard no-one saw no-one cared
and we are all its echo

Suburbia

I find myself waving back at myself
so I guess this must be a dream
I am stood in a driveway with my shirt untucked
looking for all the world like a sore loser
waving at the only man I can trust with my secrets
and the one I despise almost viscerally
a light rain is falling, dimpling the blood red dust
myself waves back with a wry smile
like someone pulling a rabbit out of a hat
it is pointless to speculate what the two of us are thinking
but there is a family stood in the middle of the street
doing just that
gazing slack-jawed at the spectacle
of me waving back at me all robe and slippers
a car speeds by and blasts its horn shrill as principle
a puppy whimpers and squirms in the little girl's arms
as the mother ferries her future to the kerb
hissing at me like the villain and his sidekick
the little girl seems to have mistaken me
for that man yelling empty promises three nights ago
from the door of a purring taxi two doors down
he wore cheap gabardine that winked in the moonlight
and seemed to have left his kind self in a mirror somewhere

Fire Stairs

or because
she lived in a profligate age
or because of something
done to her or by her

or because memory
is less a reflex than a slow broiling
and when the lights burned yellow
the rich got richer, the poor multiplied

so she kicks through the leaves
piled on the verge by a kind old widower
whose shoulders can't seem to bear
the sudden weight of her

or because there was a break in transmission
and the phone was attached to a cord
and there was a race when it rang
to tomorrow and tomorrow

or because not cruel exactly
she turns her back on the old man
brandishing his rake like an angry villager
where the seasons all seem blurred

or because
the neon lights illumine they do not reveal
and the wind prevails in strange corners of the sky
and the ghosts have all gone quiet

or because
of something done to her
or by her she
rattles each locked door on the fire stairs

laughs at the sign that reads:
THIS DOOR IS ALARMED
trapped by circumstances
only able to move in one of two directions

On the Frontier

there was no interpreter.
the last guy shot himself for reasons unknown
although we all noticed how he flinched
at even the mildest gesticulation.

there were hand signals
and the myriad triggers of a face
although in a land of bearded men
the conversations could be a little one-sided.

there was a lot of sitting around in circles
scratching at the dirt with a stick.
it is a windy country
so the conversations tended to be brief.

there were the children
who ran between us giggling
trying to read our faces
ran to tell their parents what they saw

and there were the orphans
who saw everything and were silent.

there was no interpreter to spread the news
that they had sent another interpreter from the capital
so the morning she arrived she was asked the password
(one of the many vital details absent from her brief)

she understood "password" well enough
and the sharp consonant of a gun barrel
but she was led away all the same
to some wordless space where she still languishes

like any woman with an education here
it is not so easy
to scratch "interpreter" in the dust
or the conjunction "where"

From the Wilderness

from the wilderness
comes the crack of a rifle

or maybe a tree falling
after the snow

the camp seems divided
over the source of the sound

and its direction,
it is like the north-south debate all over again.

it is noon by the time
the last peg is pulled for all the talking

and the flies so thickly by then
that one of the mules kicks hard

and snaps old Chamber's spine:
so he is shot as he mumbles Ecclesiastes

and the crack of the rifle
echoes off the hills

and the sun sets behind the stand of pines
it had risen from that morning

and one child cries and then another

Fitzgerald

I am the solipsistic agonies of Amory Blaine.
I am the Princeton night turned cold and forest-black.
I am the faces in the mist of that forest
staring back with their mouths mulling marbles.

I am the story without a by-line
about some old widower half-eaten by her cats
in a Morningside penthouse.
I am the strange feet of that dead soldier
whose ghost hides behind the curtain riddled with holes.

I am the drink that starts the day and the drink that ends it.
I am the slow dawning that they are in fact the same drink.
I am the love gone sour with too much of itself.
I am the door let off its chain to the Law's insistent gavel.
I am the agonies of Gatsby, Rosalind and Zelda.

I am a speak-easy Socrates treading the mud of the Argonne
through the shag pile hush of a lost generation.

1920 — for Tom Keneally

I must make the theatre before the curtain rises
savour the crystal chatter under Society's Very lights

before that rapid slide
to a dark watchful murmur

all the winking jewellery of the blind triumphant
amid the thud of stilettos loosed to an acre of ahhhh!

I must also remember
to carry small notes for the cabbie

save the big tips
for the Savoy maitre d

I must remember also to arch my back
as I climb the red carpet landing

to drape the fox stoll over my prosthetic arm
as the usherette clips my shaky stub

remind myself that this is not some Armentieres vaudeville
of duckboard and dead horses' tethers and army blanket

that it almost behoves a woman
to shed a quiet tear at the trill

of even the cheapest sentiment

Madame Curie

the long train ride made both Pierre and I groggy
the slow wending from the valley floor
the constant anticipation of arrival
and the thought of what we would say on stepping down.
we passed makeshift crosses from the War
like rows of crooked teeth along the dark embankment.
as it was we could barely finish a sentence on arrival
and anyway the guard stood right by our awkward gathering of
like-minds
yelling the next destination just over our heads
and I noticed his jowly face looked a little jaundiced in the
lamplight
as though he had eaten one too many railway pies
that his grey eyes welled with tears
as he yelled the names of the next three stops
and that his coat was missing a button
and his three small medals hung crooked.

*

that night we ate modishly late in a little cafe
bunched tight as battery hens in the refracted light
knees touching knees awkwardly under the black lacquered table
grinning shyly as we shovelled our opera cake.
bed beckoned and the comparative certainties of sleep
but the maid's bitch was whelping right beneath us
a full moon being the extent of any explanation or apology
we were not much liked, we sensed already
perhaps because not fluent enough
to make our gratitude sound sincere to the servants
or because we needed everything repeated like royalty.

*

by the second night the pitiful howling had stopped
and the board games grew very long and the rules difficult to follow.
I discovered a walk through the woods to a tiny lake
with a small pier and a boat moored by a frayed rope.
one of the puppies tried to follow me but lost its way in the dark
and I spent an hour trying to track its whimpering to a thorny hedge
licking its wounds amongst the foxglove and briars
its quivering stilled by my voice and my hot hands
not accustomed to lifting something so light and trusting.
I sat in the long grass and let it lick my face all over
its smooth little tongue licking away my tears
before I could even begin to explain them.
by our third night no-one had yet asked my opinion on anything.

*

on our fourth night there was a sharp disagreement in the drawing room
but the insults flew too thick and fast for me to catch them.
a quick glance at the scoring sheet suggested Bridge
which, if it hasn't already provoked a war, will soon enough.
the servants were nowhere to be seen
but the puppies bounded in as though released from somewhere
and the mood soon softened and brandies were poured
and finally someone turned to me with a serious question
about the Polish King and the Periodic Table
and I answered them to vague approval and reluctant delight
my accent, I think, this strange tremor in my voice
and a servant came to collect the puppies
which were let go with great reluctance

Aides-de-Camp

hardly
had the night ended

than she drew the curtains
to a dark storm brewing

the high thunder curling
all brassy around the curtain rings

roosting there for an hour or so
every door handle emitting an angry spark

prognosis:

two rutting away in the guest room,
two in foetal bundles on the dog leg sofa

and in an hour the delegation is due
in the sleek cars black as hearses

to sign away their country

Newsreel Ken

I liked the guy.
he smelt of rich pomade and cheap gabardine
and had a strange halting manner
when he went to shake your hand
but he smiled like he had just taken
a great bite out of the sweetest apple
and he crouched down to the kids and little dogs -
the jails are full of them -
taking time
to really look you in the eye
let you see what he's seeing
the true size and shape of us

he didn't talk much about the past
about the war or where he got that cough
although while he folded his handkerchief away
it looked for a moment like he might
just surrender to that vague
air of nostalgia that held close to him -
not cloying but close -
like the steam off a hosed down pavement

I liked the guy because of all this
and because he could fit so many marbles
into his mouth it was a wonder to behold
and when the lights went down in the cinema
he would instinctively reach out
and stroke your mother's hand
and when he looked back up at the screen
I noticed his eyes had a glassy sheen
as though he had a mouthful of marbles
almost choking on the simple joy of the moment
that you have to hold on to tight
hold on to really really tight

Palimpsest — for Tricia Dearborn

I.

sometimes
I just want to
draw a cross

and in its
left shoulder
a star

that way at least
the page
will stop staring

like that lamb
baying
at the wire.

II.

the nuns
it would seem
are more indelible

than I first gave them credit
or the living since
sorely lacking

                as they
         so sourly
              so gleefully predicted
                    over and over -

                    God's grace
          the child's sin -
                         Sisyphus and his stone.

III.

there are, they used to preach,
abundant keys to happiness,
which suggests to me there are many locks.

Still

as a child in calipers
I learnt to sleep still,
very still on my back
like the effigy on a sarcophagus
gazing up through my closed lids
beyond the night light
the dark ceiling with the faces
the damp had painted
beyond the infinite constellations
and the whispers of my parents in the other room
planning the next sermon
the next lesson in healing.

first it was my legs
and then it was my teeth:
my parents were always straightening something in me,
this crooked little boy
with his warped view of time,
of belonging,
that never got truly mended.

Mount Lofty

there is nothing
either of us
can do about it now

toasting stars
smudged out by the city
we were talking at crossed purposes

and then came
the meteor shower
and voices and lights were lowered

for the Perseids:
that strange urge to whisper
in the presence of blind agency

knowing
that this time
in a year

we will all be moving
through the same
tiny corner of space

the happy
and the sad
the living and the dead

The Seamstress

she listens to the faint trickling in the ceiling pipes
as the share rider in 4D scrubs away his nightshirt

the pipes chatter as though the shards
of a shattered glass man were being washed away up there

outside the sky brightens
the storm clouds blush as they retreat out to sea

the sea is a rumour the gulls bring to her railing
and on a warm day she thinks she can smell it

like the armpits of her mother as she sewed
gazed sadly at the piles of boxes through a cloud of nicotine

sometimes she could play for an hour in those boxes
but then she would be ordered to fill them with the night noise

the gentle whirr that lulled her to sleep
and they would eat and wait for the knock at the door

the silent exchange of one box for another:
in every package that she opens sleeps the sad smile of her mother

The Governess

I stand her facing the large bay window
because the light is good there
dappled just right by the cypress pines
and she can watch the ducks grazing on the lawn

I gather her hair
the same tincture as the light streaming through
and arrange the comb and brushes
like dinner service

she points at the glassy world and hums to herself
and knits her tiny fingers
as I run the broad comb down
ever so slowly down through her flaxen hair

and I remind her of the gardener we both watched
painting the new palings with his horsehair brush
where the pony had kicked through
spooked by the sharp booms from the quarry

one two three...we count together
all the way to twenty
counting each number off on her tiny fingers
like a dimpled abacus

then it is time for the brushing
and she arches her back a little
humming some song like a fly at the window
the summer song of all my days

she begs me not to stop
when the time comes to stop
and I smell her hair
as I lean in to tie the bow

I kiss her softly then
and the light changes with the metal scrape
of the dogs feeding below
and the hollow laughter of her mother

amongst the stable boys

St Kitts

and all the promises
the bee hums to the blushing flower

all the sly plans of butter-fed stars
the jagged architecture of wind in the leeward trees

the plantation talk of margins
and of markets that grow more distant

with each new war
each passing year

and Venus low in the east
and jungle birds sallow in the cold eye of the hurricane

and the native girls
coaxing a tune out of old rum bottles

swivelling their hips wide as morning
laughing like rain down a hillside

and all the white knuckled prayers
on the slow ride into town

grasping for a coin of sunlight on the valley floor

An Open Book

We read to know we are not alone. - C.S. Lewis

oh, where haven't I done it?

in the back seat of a Sydney cab
to the rhythmic pips of the old two-way
under De Niro's searching eye in the rear view

in bus station lavatories
in train station diners
under the fog horn of many languages
the jaundiced light of the baine-marie
and my train always lost in the mist

in sawdust tapas bars and Irish lockdowns
in the basement of damp Georgian tenements
in hotel rooms with the dripping faucet
that after a fevered night can seem like a tiny hellmouth

with a girl I barely know
who sleeps sideways on a canopied bed
who pretends to be my wife for the Belgian concierge

in a one-man tent pitched precariously
on a cliff edge above a booming sea
or in a dark German wood by Kerosene lamp
while some old god tramps its cloven hoof through the thickets

in a hatted kitchen on The Strand
while the waiters bark their orders over the glittering pass
and the dirty plates stack up
and I do it as though I had less than an hour to live

in a cramped office by torchlight
waiting for the power to come back on
waiting for the tired computers to pip alive
and the phones to start nagging again

with their stories whose moral has always eluded me

The River Man

I.

so I took a clearing lease
        off of old Curnane on the slow wend
stringybark country behind Mulgoa

        six acres pressing up against
the caky ridge
        my hand disappearing in his

as he looked me up and down
        and cocked his chin
at the bruise-blue hills

blacks up there prick worse than Welsh thistles, lad

        that was
two summers back and he and I
        have exchanged less than a torn page since

it was the last time
        I saw him smile close up
            although

he watches me plenty
        from the cobble fording
waiting to cross

        as I apply
each method as I'm
        fed them

by the kindly
	not so kindly
and the mischievous

		swinging
	axe	until
			the world

is one great echo
	ringbarking the ironbarks
		the blacks have grooved with footholds

		setting fire
	to the scrabbly
		gums further back

	away
		from the river
praying into the wind

		it
	won't change
			as it does

and the smile leaves
old Curnane's face
at his stone hearth

	I feel him
watching me plant
		by moonlight

            between
the smouldering stumps
        while the blacks' fires punch

at the bruised skin of my life now

II.

        old Curnane acquired
              the first plough
    in the district

             off a rum-red marine
    speared
                once too often

a dozen pigs
        a horse
and 20 acres of straight furrows

        lives alone
            as do I
not long

    off the stores
        I plan
to make a go of it

    Curnane
watches me sometimes
        breaking the ground with my hoe

    pitiful
as that baby possum
    I found

                        pie-eyed and screeching
        in the hollow
                of a charred stump

                    when
            I asked him
    for sow's milk

                    I knew
            I was as doomed
                            as that poor orphan

                    licking
            the milk off
                        her singed paws

                    he had a dog
                            before
                the snakes got it

it can be
        a lonely
        life

if you let it

III.

                    two nights ago
                            I woke to
                musket fire

                and a lot of blacks
with the charcoal dudgeon
        in their throats

                and a lot of white voices
       high in the throat
                     Curnane's mostly

              and three
spooked horses
              chafing at the post

IV.

            the magistrate
       is like a dog
          with a bone

the murders
      seem
            to matter less

            than the fortnight
      it took me
to bring them to light

he is my landlord
I tell him
I had my home to think of

      this does not
exactly   raise me
      in his estimation

                what made you
            venture out at all
                    he wants to know

            I heard a dog
    I tell him
            howling piteously

                a dog? a dog, sir.
                        a whole day and night
                                sir

                I thought. you thought?
        the arched brow of justice
                    in these parts

                                perhaps
                    it was caught. caught?
                        or fallen off a ledge

                        or trapped

                I am a fly
                        in his ink-black eyes
    by now
    and so
                you followed
                        the sound

                and your neighbour?
                        no trace
                        for a fortnight now

   were you armed?
     I have no gun, sir
     nor the will to aim one

  you were an army man.
  a Sergeant, sir.
  none of this sat well with him.

     I have
   a deep dread
   of the forest

  the endless dark
    of it, the
      ancient wind creaking

  I sometimes feel
    eyes
as my work

   brings me
    close
     to the ridge line

some nights
   I have dreams
     of being speared

    pinned helpless
  to the mud flats
     while they mock me

the pertinent facts please, Sergeant.
so you followed the sound?
I did sir.

                    the vivid skeleton
                        of an ox
        perched 30 feet up in the branches

                        the blacks
                    no longer warn us
                                of the coming floods

old Curnane -
your landlord -
yes, sir, my landlord he rode off

with three men -
you watched them go?
yes, sir late evening, into the hills

                        a fortnight ago
            yes sir
                            last full moon

                    and no
sign of him
            since?

                        the howling
started next morning
            with no let up

you feared the blacks?
I did sir.
and yet

                next night
                            you ventured out?
the morning after, sir

it is very dark on the ridge

                            and this
is the dog?
            I can't shake it, sir

                    uncanny looking thing
            for the record
there was a child amongst them

                            yes
                so you said:
            five men three women

and the child
and the child
and you suspect your landlord?

                    I do sir
            chasing the five into the inky night
                        half gone on rum

                        he'd been speared once
                they used to steal his maize
                            not the compromising type?

            no sir. I see.
you hear news of Mrs Hardwick
                        and the child?

                I did, sir.
    payback.
                        the child's brains

                dashed out
    just like
                        the little pickaninny's

poor defenceless woman
speared
through the throat and eyes

                I wasn't privy, sir

                        this black-eyed lord
perched
in the nook of white justice

        sends me off
with a detachment
        of twelve men

                        it is
                a slow march of twenty miles
        through the summer heat

                                we hear
the thrum of horse flies
        before we smell the bodies

The Lost Parable

there was the parable
of the fish teasing the gulls
that never got written

it began
with the soft sough of the waves
that lulled its audience to sleep

and they would dream
their disparate dreams
of dark swells and sunlight shattering on the bay

and the moral would be lost
and the fish would go back to its swimming
the gulls to their angry squawking

hovering just above the waves
on their twitching wings
as though none of the elements really wanted them

and the world would fall deeper into its habits

Acknowledgements

Poems in this collection have appeared or are forthcoming in the following publications.

Moree, Aides-de-Camp, Madame Curie, An Open Book, The Anchor, Visions of a Strawman — *Live Encounters* (Bali)
Clytemnestra, Newsreel Ken — *Verity La* (Sydney)
The Lost Parable — *Rochford Street Review* (Wentworth Falls)
Suburbia — *Stylus Poetry Journal* (Brisbane)
The Seamstress, St. Kitts, The Poet Imbibes — *In Case of Fire* (A Blue Mountains Anthology).

The Lake has also been set to music by Katoomba musician Joseph Matthews.

Milton Keynes UK
Ingram Content Group UK Ltd.
UKHW040638131024
449481UK00001B/32